How Should I Behave?

Mick Manning
and Brita Granström

FRANKLIN WATTS
LONDON·SYDNEY

Contents

How should I behave? 4

Do grown-ups always behave well? 4

So what's nice? 6

What's polite? 6

Is saying 'please' polite? 7

So 'thank you' is polite, too? 7

What's butting in? 8

What's a swear word? 8

Is it really naughty to stick out your tongue? 9

What are table manners? 10

And when I've finished eating? 11

. . . and what about burping? 11

Is farting rude, too? 12

Why should I flush the loo? 13

And do I have to wash my hands? 13

Can I pick my nose and eat my bogies? 14

And what about coughing? 15

Why should I help at home?   16

I hate queues!   18

Why's it so hard to be good at the shops?   19

What's sharing?   20

What's so good about sharing?   21

What is bullying?   22

Why do people bully?   23

Should I fight back?   23

Won't that be telling tales?   24

So it's okay to tell tales?   24

Is it bad to tell fibs?   25

What if I get lost?   26

What is 'stranger danger'?   27

But isn't that rude?   27

So how should I behave?   29

Behaving well is all about . . .   30

Index   32

How should I behave?

We should try to behave in a way we'd like other people to behave with us. You could say behaving well is 'being nice to each other'.

Do grown-ups always behave well?

No! Sadly grown-ups don't behave well all the time – just look at the news!

What we call good behaviour isn't always the
same for everyone. You might do things with
your friends that your granny would think
really cheeky. But whether it's having fun with
your mates or helping Gran find
her glasses, it's important
to be nice . . .

So what's nice?

'Nice' is a word that gets used a lot and can mean different things. It can mean being polite, being clean and tidy, or being kind and friendly.

What's polite?

When you do things to show you care about other people, you are being polite. If you're not polite, people might say you are rude or 'have bad manners'.

Is saying 'please' polite?

Yes – it is polite to say 'please' when you want something. Ask a person politely 'Please may I have ...' Then say 'thank you' when the person gives you what you asked for.

So 'thank you' is polite, too?

Yes – that's why people call them 'magic' words! They show you are not just bossy, and that you appreciate people's help or kindness. But good behaviour isn't just about magic words: it's about thinking of other people, listening to them, and not butting in when they are speaking . . .

7

What's butting in?

Interrupting when someone else is speaking! It's annoying for everyone. Listen to other people and wait until they have finished speaking before you join in or say something new.

What's a swear word?

Some words called 'swear words' are always rude. We can't say them here but if you know any – forget them! You shouldn't use words that upset other people.

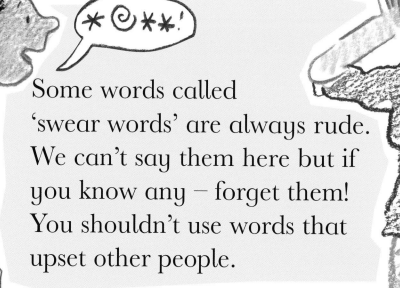

Is it really naughty to stick out your tongue?

It depends! Pulling faces can be funny sometimes as a joke with your friends, but if you do it to be nasty or to 'answer back' when you're told off, that's cheeky and bad manners.

What are table manners?

Well, at mealtimes, slurping drinks, noisy chewing, eating with your mouth open and speaking with your mouth full are all bad manners. It's good to sit still and eat carefully.

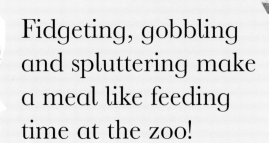

Fidgeting, gobbling and spluttering make a meal like feeding time at the zoo!

And when I've finished eating?

Don't just leave the table, ask first –
saying please, of course! And it's nice to
say 'thank you' for your meal,
even if it's just at home.

. . . and what about burping?

It's polite to burp after a
meal in some countries, but
in many others (including
this one!) people think it's
rude. So don't burp in
public and, if you
have to, cover
your mouth.

Burp!

Is farting rude, too?

When you digest your food, smelly gas builds up inside you and it's natural to let it out sometimes! But we try not to do it in front of people – they may not like the smell! Save farts for when you're on the loo . . .

Why should I flush the loo?

Do you like to find the toilet full of wee or poo? No one likes that, it attracts flies and germs – and smells horrible.

And do I have to wash my hands?

Always wash your hands after you go to the loo or before you eat to clean off dirt and germs. Germs give you tummy bugs, coughs and colds, snotty noses . . .

Can I pick my nose and eat my bogies?

No – it's dirty and not very nice for other people to watch you either. 'Bogies' are a mixture of the mucus in your nose and the dirt or germs you breathe in. They mix together and dry up to become the bogies that clog up your nostrils.

Do you really want to eat that? *Blagghh!*

14

If you've got a snotty nose, don't pick it. Blow your nose in a hanky or tissue so you don't spread germs. And throw your used tissues in the bin!

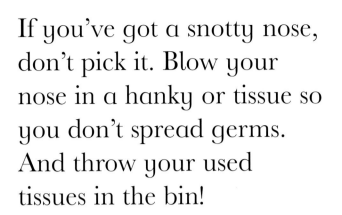

And what about coughing?

You should cover your mouth when you cough. Again it helps stop germs spreading – and no one likes someone with a cough spluttering in their face . . .

15

Why should I help at home?

Helping each other makes tidying chores go quicker. No one likes tidying – especially Mum and Dad. You can help by keeping your things tidy.

A *goal* is a team effort.

There are lots of other ways of helping. Things like helping Dad in the garden or Mum with the rubbish. It's like working in a team or a group.

A pop song is a group effort.

I hate queues!

So do we – but if we didn't queue people would just push and shove and no one would get anywhere. Queuing means everyone gets a fair turn, whether they're big or small, young or old. So don't barge in, wait your turn.

Why's it so hard to be good at the shops?

It's usually because you get bored. Shopping for food or clothes on a busy day is enough to make us all want to be cheeky monkeys! But the shopping has to be done. So try to behave well. It's another way of being helpful.

What's sharing?

Sharing is something we all have to do – at home Mum and Dad share out food. At school we share books – even teachers! We share all sorts of things; a local park or a museum is shared by everyone.

We must keep shared places clean and tidy, leaving them as we'd like to find them.

What's so good about sharing?

Sharing is a nice way to make friends. Even sharing the smallest things like your crisps or a toy makes a difference. It shows you care about other people and hope they will care about you, too . . .

What is bullying?

Bullying is picking on someone else and hurting them: punching or pulling hair, calling names or teasing. And it's not just that. Bullied children think and worry about it lots later and often don't share their fears with anyone – this can make them ill. Bullying is very cruel.

Why do people bully?

It makes them feel powerful. Very often bullies are being bullied at home, or they want to show off to their friends.

Should I fight back?

Of course you must defend yourself. But the best way to stand up to bullies is by ignoring them. If they don't stop, report them to the teacher or your parents.

Won't that be telling tales?

You should certainly tell about a bully – in fact it shows that you are braver and stronger than them if you do.

So it's okay to tell tales?

Yes, if someone is doing something dangerous or bad, then always tell a grown-up. But if your friends are just being silly and not hurting anyone, telling tales can be nasty – especially if it's a fib!

Is it bad to tell fibs?

Well, it's not good behaviour to tell even small fibs, and telling lies (big fibs) is wrong. Your friends won't like you much if you get them into trouble. And if people think you're a liar, they won't believe you any more — even when it is something really important, like there's been an accident or someone is lost . . .

Don't panic! If you get lost in a shop, ask a shop assistant for help. If you're in the street, ask someone you can trust, like a policeman or someone with children. You should know your own address and phone number.

What is 'stranger danger'?

Strangers are people we don't know. Most strangers are just like you and me, but some strangers want to hurt children. They may pretend to be nice, offering you sweets or a lift. They may say they know your parents or that they want to show you something. Ignore them and walk past quickly.

But isn't that rude?

You don't need to be polite to strangers if they frighten you! If they follow you, then walk or run towards other people, shouting out loud: 'Help me, I don't know this person.' Go in a shop and ask for help or find someone with a family of their own.

So how should I behave?

No one can be good all the time. It's not the end of the world if we get grumpy or burp loudly, and we should *always* put safety first – like shouting at friends to be careful or running away from strangers . . . But if we all try to help each other by being polite and kind and thoughtful to others, it makes life a lot fairer – and much more fun!

Behaving well is all about . . .

. . . saying please and thank you and trying not to butt in.

It's *not* about swearing, talking with your mouth full, or burping in public.

It's about keeping farts for the loo, and *not* picking your nose!

It's about remembering to flush, wash your hands, and use a hankie.

It's about helping at home and sharing things with your friends.

It's *not* about bulling or telling fibs . . .

. . . but it can be about telling tales.

It's about being aware of stranger danger.

Behaving well is all about being kind.

Index

bullying 22, 23, 24, 31
burp 10, 29, 30
butting in 7, 8, 30
cheeky 5, 9, 19
cough 15
Dad 16, 17, 20
fair 18, 29
farting 12, 30
fibs 24, 25, 31
friends 5, 6, 9, 21, 23, 24, 25, 29, 31
fun 5, 29

germs 13, 14, 15
granny 5
grown-ups 4, 24
help 5, 7, 16, 17, 19, 27, 29, 31
kind 6, 7, 29, 31
lies 25
listening 7, 8
loo 12, 13, 30
lost 25, 26
manners
  bad 6, 9, 10
  table 10-11, 30

Mum 16, 17, 20
nasty 9, 24
nice 4, 5, 6, 11, 14, 21, 27
nose picking 14, 15, 30
parents 23
please 7, 11, 30
polite 6, 7, 11, 27, 29
pulling faces 9
queue 18
rude 6, 8, 11, 27

safety 29
sharing 20, 21, 22, 31
shopping 19, 26
strangers 27, 29, 31
swearing 8, 30
teachers 20, 23
team 16
teasing 22
telling tales 24, 31
thank you 7, 11, 30
tidy 6, 16, 21
wash 13, 30

For Max and Björn who behave very well – most of the time!

First published in 2002
by Franklin Watts,
96 Leonard Street,
London EC2A 4XD

Franklin Watts Australia
56 O'Riordan Street
Alexandria
NSW 2015

The illustrations in this book have been drawn by Brita

Text and illustrations © 2002
Mick Manning and Brita Granström

Series editor: Rachel Cooke
Art director: Jonathan Hair

Printed in Hong Kong, China
A CIP catalogue record is available from the British Library.

Dewey Classification 395
ISBN 0 7496 3998 9